Chinese Pioneering Inventions Series

The Great Wall

Edited by Li Chaodong

Translated by Xuemeng Angela Li

RC

Books Beyond Boundaries

ROYAL COLLINS

In a nature full of dangers, animals use different methods to protect themselves.

Little ants use soil to build "yards."

Zokors dig "luxury suites" underground.

Bees create delicate houses.

These small animals know how to protect themselves. How do we humans protect ourselves?

Birds cut holes in trees as their homes.

Human built high fences to protect themselves and their families.

To safeguard their cities,
they also built walls.

Then, what do people use to protect their country?

The Great Wall enables the Chinese people to live and prosper continuously.

Beacon Tower: It is used for transmitting military information. (It uses smoke by day and fire by night as signals.)

The current version of the Great Wall that we see is not original. In the beginning, there were only beacon towers without a connected wall.

In ancient times, there was no telephone; how did people transmit military information?

When enemies came to intrude, people lit smoke during the day and fire at night on the beacon, one after another, to deliver the news of the appearance of enemies.

Later, in order to transmit information more accurately, people also established a beacon system.

During the Spring and Autumn and the Warring States Periods, many vassal states built their own state wall to protect their territories.

In the north: Three states, including Qin, Zhao, and Yan, built walls to defend themselves against invaders.

In the south: The warring vassal states all built their own state walls to defend themselves against the power of each other.

Among all states, Qin gradually grew in power. Qin Shi Huang (the first emperor of Qin) eventually unified the vassal states to the east. After unification, the new Qin Dynasty dismantled all the scattered state walls and connected all vassal states by building roads.

At the same time, in response to the harassment and plundering of the Xiongnu people from the north, the people of Qin began to build a new wall based on the old state walls in northern Zhao and Yan. After Meng Tian (A famous military general of the Qin Dynasty) repelled the Xiongnu people, he led 300,000 generals, soldiers, and a large number of civilians to build the Great Wall.

The Qin Dynasty spent enormous labor and resources on building the Great Wall, which made its people live on the edge of starvation. At the end of the Qin Dynasty, a large-scale peasant rebellion broke out. The leader of the rebellion, Liu Bang, won the battle eventually and established the Han Dynasty.

During the Han Dynasty, the great general Huo Qubing attacked the Xiongnu people towards the west and took over the Hexi Corridor. As a result, the Han Dynasty established Wuwei and Jiuquan Counties and kept building the Great Wall along the Hexi Corridor.

Later, the Han Dynasty established Zhangye County and Dunhuang County and began building the Great Wall between Jiuquan and Yumen Pass (Jade Gate).

After Emperor Wu of Han sent Li Guangli (A military general of the Western Han Dynasty whose family was favored by Emperor Wu of Han) to conquer Dayuan, the Great Wall between the west of Dunhuang and Lop Nur was also built.

In the desert, the generals and their soldiers had no access to stone, so they built the Great Wall using local gravel and tree branches.

During peaceful times, Han Dynasty soldiers established military markets in the frontier regions and traded with the Xiongnu people using grain, silk, and tea leaves in exchange for their fur and cattle. Big merchants from the Central Plains also conducted trade with the people.

At the same time, the Han Dynasty also implemented a new migration policy for its northern border to train the people who lived there. Border residents cultivated the farmland regularly in peacetime. But when the enemy attacked, they used weapons to defend their homes. Their self-sufficient production method not only saved the state large amounts of money in military expenses but also contributed to local agriculture and economic development (It is also called an agricultural colony).

Under the protection of the Great Wall, the Hexi Corridor became increasingly lively, further advancing the Silk Road's development. Communications between the Han Dynasty and Central Asia also became increasingly frequent.

The Great Wall not only improved the peace and stability of border areas but also guaranteed the prosperity of the Sui and Tang dynasties.

Jiayu Pass

Qinghai

Inner Mongolia

Beijing

Tian

Heibei

Shanxi

Shaan'xi

Gansu

Liaoning

Hushan

The existing Great Wall was built mainly during the Ming Dynasty. While Ming was building the Great Wall in its north, it also moved its capital from Nanjing to Beijing, closer to its border.

Both the construction technologies and defensive performance of the Ming Great Wall reached the top level. Improvements in its building materials and construction methods led to higher solidity of the wall. At the same time, the use of horse faces and passageways increased the defending performance of the Great Wall.

Near Loess Plateau, people normally source construction materials locally. They built kilns to bake bricks and constructed the wall by covering blue bricks outside and ramming loess inside.

In addition to the materials, the structure of the Ming Great Wall has also been strengthened.

Parapet: It is used to prevent soldiers and carriages from falling.

Battlement: It is used to observe and attack enemies.

The wall is normally four or five meters wide and can accommodate four horses abreast. It facilitates force maneuver and the transportation of food and weapons during the battle.

Battlement

Parapet

At intervals, there is a protruding platform on the wall called the "horse face." It allows soldiers to attack enemies interchangeably from both its front and side.

One man guards the pass, ten thousand cannot break through.

Jiayu Pass

It is the pass at the west end of the Ming Great Wall, the strategic passage of Hexi Corridor, and the transportation hub of the ancient "Silk Road." It is also one of the three wonders of the Great Wall of China. (The Shanhai Pass in the east, the Zhen Bei Tai Tower in the middle, and the Jiayu Pass in the west.)

Juyong Pass

Known as "The Most Impregnable Pass in the World," Juyong Pass is the oldest and most famous pass of the Great Wall of China.

Yanmen Pass

It is famous for being "dangerous." It is said that "Yanmen is the top out of all nine fortresses in China." It is one of the "Three Outer Passes," along with Ningwu Pass and Pianguan Pass.

Shanhai Pass

It is located where the Great Wall meets the sea and is called "The Top Pass in the World."

Outside the passes of some larger cities; a smaller city would also be developed, known as the barbican (urn city). As the saying goes, "A small city is like an urn where one can catch a turtle inside." When enemies enter the barbican, the guards will attack them from all directions.

During the Qing Dynasty, the original Great Wall, which had been used to defend invaders, was dismantled. The isolation it created between both sides was broken.

The Qing Dynasty also built temples to promote Buddhism and consolidate its rule through ideology and culture.

Although wars took place frequently on both sides during ancient times, the Great Wall provided a platform for the communication and trade between nomadic and agrarian peoples over the centuries, promoting the cultural integration of Han and minorities, which eventually formed the Chinese culture.

In addition, the Great Wall prevented nomads from moving down south, forcing them to conquer the west and thus changed the historical course of Eurasia.

Chinese Pioneering Inventions Series

The Great Wall

Edited by Li Chaodong
Translated by Xuemeng Angela Li

First published in 2023 by Royal Collins Publishing Group Inc.
Groupe Publication Royal Collins Inc.
BKM Royalcollins Publishers Private Limited

Headquarters: 550-555 boul. René-Lévesque O Montréal (Québec) H2Z1B1 Canada
India office: 805 Hemkunt House, 8th Floor, Rajendra Place, New Delhi 110 008

Original Edition © Hohai University Press

ISBN: 978-1-4878-1100-6

To find out more about our publications, please visit www.royalcollins.com.

About the Editor

Li Chaodong, born in 1963, graduated from the Department of History of East China Normal University. He is a famous education publisher in China. He has edited and published more than 50 sets of books. He has won the title of "National Leading Talent in Press and Publication" and "China's Annual Publication Figure." He is the Founding Vice President of the All-China Federation of Industry and Commerce Book Industry Chamber of Commerce, Vice President of the Fifth Council of China Book Publishing Association, Vice Chairman of Anhui Publishing Association, and Vice Chairman of Jiangsu Publishing Association.